MISS

Great Snakes!

Kit Wright

Great Snakes!

Illustrated by Posy Simmonds

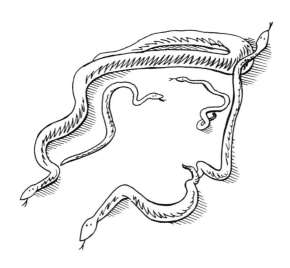

VIKING

VIKING

Published by the Penguin Group
Penguin Books Ltd, 27 Wrights Lane, London w8 5TZ, England
Penguin Books USA Inc., 375 Hudson Street, New York, New York 10014, USA
Penguin Books Australia Ltd, Ringwood, Victoria, Australia
Penguin Books Canada Ltd, 10 Alcorn Avenue, Toronto, Ontario, Canada M4V 3B2
Penguin Books (NZ) Ltd, 182–190 Wairau Road, Auckland 10, New Zealand

Penguin Books Ltd, Registered Offices: Harmondsworth, Middlesex, England

First published 1994
10 9 8 7 6 5 4 3 2 1

Text copyright © Kit Wright, 1994
Illustrations copyright © Posy Simmonds, 1994

The moral right of the author and illustrator has been asserted

Filmset in Linotron Plantin by
Rowland Phototypesetting Ltd, Bury St Edmunds, Suffolk

Made and printed in Great Britain by
Butler and Tanner Ltd, Frome, Somerset

A CIP catalogue record for this book is available from the British Library

ISBN 0–670–83093–3

What is a book of verse without
A dedication at the front?
It's like a pig without a snout
To guide it on a truffle hunt.
Let's therefore hope that *FINBAR WRIGHT*
Will find things here for his delight!

Contents

The Very First People on Earth

Did the very first people on earth rejoice
At being the earth's first people?

They did not.

They stood about kicking at lumps of flint
And sneered at their situation.

'Why hasn't Concorde been invented?' they
                                              cried.
'Then we could get
The hell out of here.'

And 'You can't even get a cup of tea!' they
                                            moaned.
And 'Why is that mammoth mammoth
Glowering from that rock?

'Why is that mammoth mammoth
Glowering from that rock?

'Why is that mammoth ma–'

The Man Who Invented Football

The man who invented football,
He must have been dead clever,
He hadn't even a football shirt
Or any clothes whatever.

The man who invented soccer,
He hadn't even a *ball*
Or boots, but only his horny feet
And a bison's skull, that's all.

The man who invented football,
To whom our hats we doff,
Had only the sun for a yellow card
And death to send him off.

The cave-mouth was the goal-mouth,
The wind was the referee,
When the man who did it did it
In 30,000 BC!

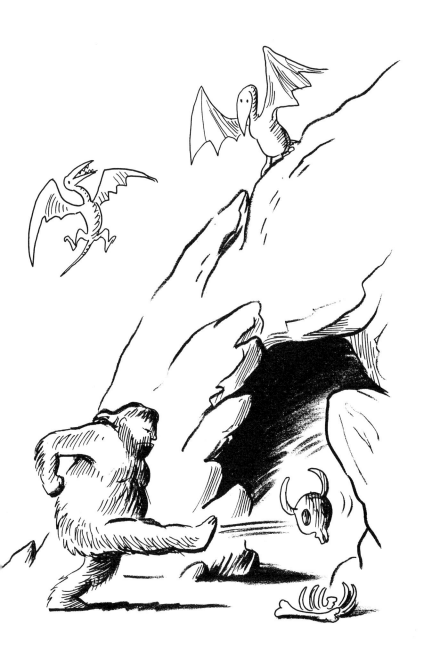

The Balham Alligator

If you walk up Balham High Road
And you wander down a by-road
To the common and the woods
That lie beyond,

You will meet if you are patient there
An animal that's stationed there,
An alligator living
In the pond . . .

He's the BALHAM ALLIGATOR on the run,
                              run, run,
And he's hiding from his Keeper
In the Zoo!

To the Zoo he took a scunner
Which is why he done a runner
And he's waiting there
Just for
You!

So if you care to stay with him
And pass the time of day with him
And have a heart-to-heart there
One to one,

(That's if you've got the bottle)
He will like it quite a lottle,
Will the Balham Alligator
On the run!

Oh, the BALHAM ALLIGATOR on the run, run,
                                            run,

They took him from the swamp
Across the sea,

And he found his new home horrider
In every way than Florida
And that's how
He comes to
Be . . .

The . . .

BALHAM ALLIGATOR on the run, run, run!
Oh, he's hiding from his Keeper
In the Zoo!

To the Zoo he took a scunner
Which is why he done a runner
And he's waiting there
Just for
You!

Watch out.

The Woodman's Axe

The old woodman had only one axe,
a true axe and a keen one.
He swung it in the oakwood
all day long.

When the handle split he fitted another.
When the blade cracked he fitted another.
He passed it on to his son,
who swung it in the oakwood
all day long.

Blade and handle, handle and blade,
he fitted as he needed.

A man said, 'What is left of the axe
whose parts have changed so many times?'

But the son said, 'I have only one axe
passed on to me by my father:
a true axe and a keen one.'

And he passed it on to his son.

What Went Wrong at My Sister's Wedding

The bridegroom was supposed
To kiss the bride,
Not kick 'er

And

He shouldn't have kissed
The Vicar

And

They should have thrown
Confetti,
Not

Spaghetti.

Deena the Rain Queen

The summer sky was a misery,
*   All heavy and dull and numb,*
With all the charm of a broken arm
*   Or a sumo wrestler's bum.*

Clouds, they queued over Cambridge
*   Like trucks in a traffic jam*
And never a ripple there came to stipple
*   The washed-up River Cam*

When

Deena Patel came by!
Deena Patel came by!

Now,

Deena Patel
Is a girl I know well
And she isn't a creature
That stays in its shell:
A helluva person
Is Deena Patel!

She grabbed the sky
By a couple of corners
And shook it out
And banged it down
On the iron earth
And those weary mourners,
The clouds, she booted
All over the town . . .
Till thunder lifted
One ear and growled
And lightning whiplashed
And mad winds moaned
And greylight shifted
For hurtling darkening:
Ground and river
The rainstorm stoned!

And afterwards in the evening
The sun came out to see
The grateful green and freshened sheen
Of each sparkling, dripping tree.

So whenever the sky's a misery
Under a baleful spell
Or a sick, grey curse, you could do worse
Than . . . SEND FOR DEENA PATEL!

Rock Around the Wok

There's a frying and a frizzling
      and a simmer and a sizzling
      in the WOK . . .

There's a bunch o' crazy beanshoots
      and the shoots are pretty meanshoots
      in the WOK . . .

There's a ginger root a-jumping
      and a lotta stalks a-stumping
      in the WOK . . .

There's onions that are springing
   and there's flavours that are singing
   in the WOK . . .

   So,
   Baby,

   LET'S GO STIR THE WOK
   (Oh, baby)
   LET'S GO STIR THE WOK
   (Oh, baby)
   ROCK AROUND THE WOK

Because:

There's a lotta food,
    There's a lotta heat.
So shake it up!
    That's enough.
    Let's eat

FROM THE WOK!

The Publishing Puffin

A puffin on her native cliff
Above the breakers foaming white
Spied in the rock a hieroglyph
And read it with immense delight.
Her mind's eye took a photostat.
'I think,' she said, 'I'll publish that.'

And publish it she did indeed,
As also works of guillemots
And terns, and every other breed
Of sea-bird in the coastal spots,
Until word sped of her on land
And human songs she took in hand.

And that is why this very day
Above those crags and hollowed crypts
People queue with things to say,
Authors bearing manuscripts,
Hoping that they might bring joy
To sea-bird, or to girl or boy.

Waiting for the Tone

My sister is my surest friend
And yet, GREAT SNAKES! she seems to spend
Her *life* upon the telephone
Talking to her boyfriend, Tone,
Although – a sad and sorry joke –
She doesn't seem to *like* the bloke.

> *'Don't take that tone with me, Tone,*
> *Don't take that tone with me,*
> *Or else I'll put down the phone, Tone,*
> *And alone, Tone, you will be.*
>
> *'Don't call me just to moan, Tone,*
> *Can't stand your whingeing on.*
> *Next time you ring for a groan, Tone,*
> *You'll find that I have gone.'*

And she can keep this up for hours:
Her taste for Tone's moans never sours.
So when I think that he might call
I silently steal down the hall
And give the phone a hateful look . . .
Then take the blighter off the hook.

Uncle Know-all

He knows what's what,
He knows what's not,
He knows that never
The twain shall meet.
He knows his onions,
He knows his bunions,
He knows his nose
And he knows his feet.

He knows his mind,
He knows his value,
Knows what happens,
Knows how it goes.
He knows the lot
And doesn't he love it,
I wish he'd shove it
Up his nose!

Twist

There wasn't a fellow named Twist,
Which is good, for he'll never be missed.
   He did not a thing.
   Well, he couldn't. The sting
Is this limerick doesn't exist.

Well Done, George

The poet George MacBeth possessed
The worst handwriting in the West.
It looked like smuts discharged by fire,
Or argumentative barbed wire,
Or bracken trampled in a wood.
You get the point. It wasn't good.

And yet the words he wrote were rare
And splendid and beyond compare.
Lucky for us, he typed them out
So no one had the slightest doubt,
When they were printed in a book,
That they were *really* worth a look!

So if your scrawl's a scrum or splatter,
Nest of nostril hairs, no matter.
Think of George, who couldn't get
The letters of his *name* to set,
And practise WELL DONE, GEORGE because
A nicer man there never was.

When the Pope Takes a Shower

Should the Pope
grope
for the soap,
and the soap
slip off the slope,
would the Pope
feel a dope,
would hope
be beyond his scope,
would the Pope
mope?

Nope.
The Pope
could cope.

In Cold Blood

Some snakes are secrets
that issue themselves from shadows
and spoon their heads onwards to follow
their forking tongues

in a system of S's,
successively slithering silently,
always on oil, and wrapping
their rings round rungs.

They never stop growing
and when they need roomier garments
they wrestle their skins off and dump them
inside out.

They bite their way free
from eggs like spuds or parsnips.
Fangs are a kettle of venom's
double spout.

Some eat each other,
and some will consume a whole leopard,
then fast for a year, while some
can swallow a goat.

Some get a crush
on a creature and squeeze its heart
till it slides down the long canal
like a narrow boat.

None vegetarian,
many are wonderfully beautiful,
jewel-ropes of green
and copper and gold

on tree, grass, rock,
in the sea. They have their sorrows,
and die if they ever eat anything
too cold . . .

The Jellyfish Reunion

Two old jellyfish

who hadn't seen each other
for *years*

wobbled and hobbled
and hobbled and wobbled
over a lumpety
bumpety beach
to meet for a chat
and a snifter
of seaweed
after all that
time.

What's new with you?
Not much. And you?
Not much with me.

So two old jellyfish

who wouldn't see each other
for *years*

hobbled and wobbled
and wobbled and hobbled
back over the lumpety
bumpety beach

and snuggled
into the sea.

Sprout
(for Laurel and Hardy)

On the long road leading out of Cambridge,
On the trail of the loathsome sprout . . .

When the sun was out,
I tweaked your snout.
You said I was a person
You could do without.

Oh, March,

Where potatoes have the starch,
Not the sprout!

I'm so loathsome to you-hoo!

On the long road leading out of Cambridge,
On the trail of the loathsome sprout!

Monty Makes It

Monty was a Mountie on the plains of Manitoba,
He was very seldom saddled, he was very seldom
                                                   sober,
And they murmured round the province and
                            across Sas-kat-chew-*an*
That Monty was a Mountie
Who *never* got his man.

Woody was a dog-thief working down in old
                                        Toronto,
He was hounded, he was hunted, so he left
                                  Toronto pronto
And he headed for the prairies where grain-
                                elevators rise
For he figured he'd lie *doggo*
Beneath those mammoth skies.

Now Monty gets to snoozing after far too much
libation.
Outside the little tavern snores the owner's huge
Alsatian
When there comes a gravel growling and a
yelping and a yowl.
Up awake springs Monty.
'A dog-thief's on the prowl!'

The moment Woody catches that, he thinks he'd
best skedaddle.
Out the bar reels Monty and he leaps up for the
saddle,
But he doesn't just quite make it though he never
hits the ground.
No, coming down like thunder,
He lands *astride the hound*!

Which takes off like a blizzard through the miles
of standing wheat
With Monty hanging on by all his elbows, chin
and feet,
And the guys inside the tavern, well, they rate his
chances slim.
'Say goodbye to Monty.
Last we seen of him!'

So what's become of Woody? Well, he's figuring
                                                to sneak
Inside a big red barn that stands beside a winding
                                                creek,
When he turns and, to his horror, his dismay and
                                                consternation,
There's Monty coming at him.
He's back – on the Alsatian!

It's looking bad for Woody. What to do now,
                              where to hide?
He staggers back, forgetting he's beside the
                              waterside,
Which might not be disastrous nor his prospects
                              quite so dim
Except for just one detail:
Woody cannot swim!

Now Monty's had a drink or two, the dog has not
                              had one,
So it's dusty, hot and thirsty from the circuit it
                              has run
And it races for the water like a living lightning
                              streak.
Splash! Ker-rash! Ker-rikey!
It jumps into the creek.

So poor old Woody's sinking for the third time
out of view.
Monty hauls him out and puts him on the dog's
back too
And they flounder from the water and they gallop
from the shore,
Till, bounding from the wheatfield,
They hit the tavern door!

The charge? Attempted dog-theft, and old
Woody has confessed.
The guys inside the tavern, they say, 'Monty,
we're impressed.'
So they murmur round the province and across
Sas-kat-chew-*an*

That Monty is a Mountie
Who ONE TIME GOT HIS MAN!

I Heard Someone Crying

I heard someone crying
A long way off. I was going

Down Sampson Street. I was hoping
My sister would be staying.

She's living
A long way off from us, she's working

Somewhere else. That evening,
Coming

Home from school, I was turning
The key when I heard her laughing

And then she was kissing
My face and we were hugging

And tumbling. Who was crying
On Sampson Street?

Reaching a Watershed

Reaching a watershed,
she sat at a water-table
and drank a glass of water.
Then, after she had eaten
a watermelon with watercress,
she painted a watercolour
of Derwent Water
with water wagtails
in a watery sky
and water-rats
in the waterweed.
She stared at it. It made her eyes

weep. It was
a washout.

The Water Waiter

As we sit at our table by the sea,
again and again the clumsy old waiter,
the dumbo, clumsy old water waiter,
rolls up with his tray of undrinkable drinks
again and again and every time
falls head over head over head over heels with it
every time and thank you for trying,
waiter.

Fair Warning of a Goddess

She can change her shape
To a snake or a sparrow,
With a silver arrow
Shoot down the moon:
She can tickle the sun
Awake at night-time,
Tip over darkness
Into noon.

She'll come yesterday,
She was here tomorrow,
She can bend and borrow
Whale words from the sea:
With one big toe
She can stop a river
Dead, then hang it
Up on a tree.

She can spin the world
On a single finger
And make life linger
Or let it go:
She can char the sky
With a wedding torch
Or from one dead branch
Make a forest grow:

If you should meet her
In TAMILNADU,
Don't say I didn't ever
Tell you so . . .

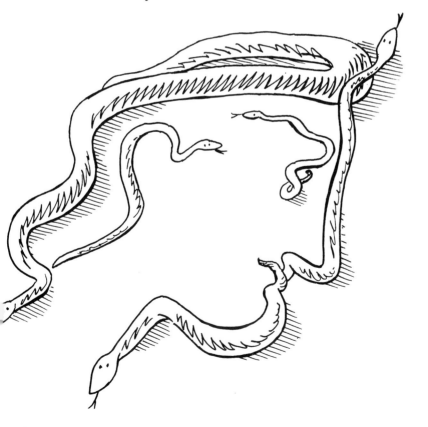

Mariannagram

The happiest discovery
Of all her life and times?
The MERRY CHRISTMAS anagram
Of MR STARRYCHIMES!

The Tears of Things

When cows are cowed
and sheep
are sheepish

in the deep
they feel it
deepish.

How they mourn
for each
landlubber.

Fish sing scales
of grief.
Whales

blubber.

Spooky Sentence

Outside was blind with mist till the grey turned
                                                         darker
and swung its shadows from the beams

in the strange kitchen
where the old woman

sat with her head so low
between her pointy shoulders,

her chin was scooping for something I could not
                                                            see
in the darkness lit by a tooth

and her grin
creaked . . .

A Little Night Music

I lay awake at midnight
And a smile was on my face
As I heard the caterwauling
Of the cats in Feline Place.
They were bawling, they were yowling,
And they yodelled at the moon.

I grinned a grin: for *my* cat
Was the *only* cat in tune!

I sprang awake at 5 a.m.
The dogs in Canine Square
Were barking out a Bach Chorale
And barking mad they were.
They angered all the neighbourhood
And terrified the birds.

I grinned a grin: for *my* dog,
And *he only*, knew the words!

So

Tickle my funny-bone nightly,
Tickle my funny-bone, do!
You can't get bamboo shoots at Boots
But you can get Boots shampoo –

Oi!

Fenby

November hung its head in gloom
When Fenby led us to his room.

He sat us down and right away
Announced to all who cared to stay:

'I cannot undertake to state
A single thing. I can't relate

'One episode of all of time.
I cannot fall. I cannot climb.

'I cannot break. I cannot mend.
I can't begin. I cannot end.

'I cannot name the reason why
I cannot live but cannot die.'

'Bad luck!' said someone, maybe me,
And wondered if a cup of tea

Was totally beyond his powers.
'I can't. I cannot count the hours

'I've failed to make the tea-bag swim.
I cannot bring it to the brim.'

At which I heard an oldster call:
'CAN YOU DO ANYTHING AT ALL

'OF ANY USE IN ANY WAY?'
And Fenby said: 'I cannot say.'

The Fall of Cleopatra

Three in a tree-house,
tree-house trio,
up in an ash
with a dog named Cleo.

Two were girls
and one was a fella
and the loudest child was
Isabella.

The dog fell off
their sky-borne raft
and Isabella
laughed &
    "   &
    "   &
    "   &
    "   &
    "   &
    "   &
    "   &

felt a bit sick.

A Bit of Luck for Sonia

I wish you were sunnier, Sonia,
I wish you'd the happiness knack.
I wish you kept saying, 'Good on yer!'
And giving me pats on the back.

But wishes are wasted upon yer,
For chumminess never you'll learn,
So, Sonia, I'm off to Bologna,
And don't think I'll ever return!

Incident on the Island

Once upon the Isle of Thanet
I was sitting by the sea
When a gull, or else a gannet,
Landed something on my knee.

By my side my old friend Janet
Loudly laughed at my mishap.
What an island! What a planet!
What a way to treat a chap!

Guide-dog Blues

Howling city high road or rutted country track,
If the harness be a-straining, or if the reins be
                                        slack,
Dog here, boss, right with you: take you by hell
                                        and back.

Dog here, boss, through the winter's slithery
                                slush and slime,
Eyes for you in the springtime leafing of beech
                                and lime:
But why do we never seem to want to pee at the
                                same time?

The Rotters

From early enough in the morning
Till moon made its mark,
Mr and Mrs Rotter
Sat on a bench in the park.

Side by side, most dearly,
They were their favourite friends,
Candles that lit each other
Down to the candle-ends.

When sky was terracotta,
Baked in the late sun's ray,
Mr and Mrs Rotter
Held hands at the end of the day.

When pond-bank sun like an otter
Slid in out of sight,
Mr and Mrs Rotter
Kissed at the birth of night.

The last words that they whispered
Tenderly, stars above?
'My dear, you are a Rotter!'
'And so are you, my love!'

Twist Two

Remember old Twist who was not?
I've just had more news and it's hot.
  He's *still* to arrive!
  Is he frit? Does he skive?
Is he timid, or idle, or what?

Arnos Grove

Arnos Grove is a London neighbourhood,
Arnos Grove is a place to go,
Arnos Grove is a kind community,
Oldsters smile there, young ones grow.

Arnos Grove means a different thing to me,
Arnos Grove seems a shortish chap
In a small tweed hat with a feather tucked in it,
All of his friendliness there on tap.

I shall go with the evening Londoners,
Dusk be purple or dusk be mauve,
I shall walk till the end of everything
Down with Arnos through the Grove.

Cheering Up Ivan

When Catherine the Great met Ivan the Terrible
Down at the old Pier Head,

It was, 'How are you, Cath?'
'I'm great! And you?'
'Terrible,' Ivan said.

'Cheer up, son! We'll phone William the Silent.
He'll know what to do.

Bill, is that you?
Bill, is that you?
Bill?'

The Chap

I happened once to know a chap:
You may have known him too –

But only, of course, if your chap's name
Was in every way the very same
As the name of the chap I knew.

But if by the merest whisker
Those names are out of line,

Then my chap, poor chap, wasn't your chap,
Your chap wasn't mine!

All of Us

All of us are afraid
More often than we tell.

There are times we cling like mussels to the sea-
                                               wall,
And pray that the pounding waves
Won't smash our shell.

Times we hear nothing but the sound
Of our loneliness, like a cracked bell
From fields far away where the trees are in icy
                                               shade.

O many a time in the night-time and in the day,
More often than we say,
We are afraid.

If people say they are never frightened,
I don't believe them.
If people say they are frightened,
I want to retrieve them

From that dark shivering haunt
Where they don't want to be,
Nor I.

Let's make of ourselves, therefore, an enormous
                                              sky

Over whatever
We most hold dear.

And we'll comfort each other,
Comfort each other's
Fear.

A Day at the Races

Edward Woodward went to Goodwood
  Every time he could.
If Edward Woodward could make Goodwood,
  Edward Woodward would,

  Would Woodward.

Once he put a lot of bunce
  Upon a wild grey mare.
Instead of trackward, it went backward,
  Edward didn't care!

  No,

Edward Woodward went to Goodwood
  Every time he could.
If Edward Woodward could make Goodwood,
  Edward Woodward would.

This

Jolly good actor, then he backed a
   Sorrel running *yet*!
Did Edward quarrel with the sorrel?
   No, he didn't fret!

Oh,

Edward Woodward went to Goodwood
   Every time he could.
If Edward Woodward could make Goodwood,
   Edward Woodward would!

(Would Woodward?)

75

The Sea in the Trees

When the warm wind was flowing
In the leaves of the tall ash tree,
The old man fell asleep in the park
And he dreamed the sound of the sea.

The branches filled and billowed,
The high mainmast swayed,
As long sea-miles of the afternoon
His green galleon made . . .

In the harbour of the shade.

Not Known at This Address

I decided to ask my friends to write,
If ever they would, instead of just
Talk talk talk,

To:

THE DEPARTMENT OF HUMAN
                    GENIUS,
CENTRE OF WORLD EXCELLENCE,
73 MILL WALK.

And one of them
Actually did. My mum
Had carefully placed the envelope
On the windowsill.
She said:

'That seems to be for you.
I think it's a bill.'

Gary the Great

Watching cricket one June day
When folk in sunlight basked,
I wandered round the boundary
Until I stopped and asked
An old man who'd made many Junes
And many sad Octobers,
'Who was the best you ever saw?'
He said, *'Sir Garfield Sobers.*

'Sir Gary was the best of all
Who could both strike and bowl a ball.
In few the twin arts marry,
But since you're looking for a name
That honours most this funny game,
My friend, I give you Gary.

'He bowled fast-medium or slow,
He hit six sixes in a row,
That's quite a way to carry:
And every run he ever made
Seemed effortless. The ball obeyed
His bat: I give you Gary.'

I walked away. He called me back.
'Friend, cricket is a *live* scene,
And younger ones will make more tons –
He's just the best one *I've* seen!'

Home and Dry

Upon the street down which I stride
Rain springs as off a trampoline.
The sky's enormous tear-machine
Creates a swirling inland tide.

But just the other day I bought
A spanking, sparkling new umbrella,
Canopy of blue and yeller,
Broad and deep and strong and taut.

So do I worry? Yes. And why?
My smug new brolly's home and dry.

(PS *I am a clever fellow
And know the proper word is* yellow.)

Candy and Joe

Candy and Joe lived hand-to-mouth
   And yet saw eye-to-eye.
They were neck-and-neck in their love for each
                                  other
   Till the sweet old by-and-by.

They were hand-in-glove till push came to shove,
And it got to the old no-go:

LADIES AND GENTS,
THEY WERE EXCELLENT PEOPLE,

LET'S HEAR IT
FOR CANDY AND JOE!

Naturally

Some big elephant
lumbered on the high savannah

by the great grass plains
and the new blue sky,

nudging along her
calf before her

with her great grey body
and her ancient eye.

Some big elephant
wallowed out into the water-hole,

trumpeted and hosed
till the bath was done.

'What's that, Daddy?'
said the baby in the car.

'That's

some

big

elephant,

son!'

The Sympathetic Rats

York Minster was troubled with rats.
They were driving the Archbishop bats.
  (One daredevil blighter
  Ran right down his mitre
And bit a chunk out of his spats!)

  So he said to the Dean,
    'Well, I just about *died*!
What on earth can we do?'
    And the Dean, he replied:

'I'm getting a firm in from Kidderminster
Who really *do* know how to ridderminster
  Of all kinds of pest.
  They're the tops, they're the best!
But they charge about five thousand
               quidderminster.

'That's quite a big chunk
    Of episcopal dough
And how we shall raise it
    I really don't know.'

Then the Archbishop broke down and cried.
The sight *put the rats on his side*!
    They held a tombola
    And raised the payola
And paid for the poison – and died!

The Water-trumpet Voluntary:
A Nasty Piece of Work

Upon the water-trumpet once
A lonely man in Greenland played,
And passionate was his lament
And angry were the blues he made.
Beside him on the snow-trombone
A vampire flowered for a while:
Then winter sun came out and splayed
The evil oven of its smile.

Twist Three

Great news! Twist's at last taken place
And it seems she's a woman named Grace!
   She took a dim view
   Of the world and withdrew,
So Grace Twist's disappeared without trace!

Index of first lines

What is a book of verse without
A dedication at the back?
It's like a pig without a tail,
Or like a snail without a track.
So we have one thing left to do:
Let's dedicate this book . . . to YOU!